Contents

Where does this glow-in-the-dark mushroom grow?

Find out on page 22!

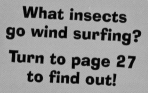

What insects go wind surfing?

Turn to page 27 to find out!

Some words are shown in bold, **like this**. These words are explained in the glossary. You will find important information and definitions underlined, <u>like this</u>.

THE Living PLaneT

The planet Earth is full of living things. Life can be found almost everywhere you look. It is in the depths of the oceans and in the heart of the desert. Life also comes in many different shapes and forms. How can we make sense of it all?

Humans have always taken an interest in the huge variety of plants and animals around them. Thousands of years ago, that interest was a matter of survival. It was important to know what we could catch and eat, and how to avoid being eaten or poisoned.

FINDING OUT MORE

Eventually we wanted to know more about living things than simply which were tasty and which were dangerous. Scientists began to try and make sense of how one living thing was related to another. They wondered how living things actually worked, and why they behaved the way they do.

Many people have taken a great deal of time and effort to unravel these mysteries. It is a task that continues to this day and there is no end in sight. The living world is a rich and complex one.

The Scientists Behind
Living Things

Robert Snedden

www.raintreepublishers.co.uk
Visit our website to find out more information about Raintree books.

To order:
☎ Phone 0845 6044371
📄 Fax +44 (0) 1865 312263
✉ Email myorders@raintreepublishers.co.uk

Customers from outside the UK please telephone +44 1865 312262

Raintree is an imprint of Capstone Global Library Limited, a company incorporated in England and Wales having its registered office at 7 Pilgrim Street, London, EC4V 6LB – Registered company number: 6695582

Text © Capstone Global Library Limited 2011
First published in hardback in 2011
Paperback edition first published in 2012
The moral rights of the proprietor have been asserted.

Edited by Andrew Farrow, Adam Miller, and Diyan Leake
Designed by Philippa Jenkins
Original illustrations © Capstone Global Library Limited 2011
Illustrated by Capstone Global Library Limited and Ian Escott
Picture research by Hannah Taylor
Originated by Capstone Global Library Limited
Printed and bound in China by CTPS

ISBN 978 1 406 22060 5 (hardback)
14 13 12 11 10
10 9 8 7 6 5 4 3 2 1

ISBN 978 1 406 22188 6 (paperback)
15 14 13 12 11
10 9 8 7 6 5 4 3 2 1

British Library Cataloguing in Publication Data
Snedden, Robert
  The scientists behind living things. -- (Sci-hi)
  570.9'22-dc22
A full catalogue record for this book is available from the British Library.

Acknowledgements
The author and publisher are grateful to the following for permission to reproduce copyright material: Alamy Images pp. **17** (© Dynamic Light USA), **21** (© John Glover), **26** (© Chris Mattison), **34** (© Aurora Photos); The Art Archive p. **20**; Suz Bateson p. **11** (Biodiversity Institute of Ontario (BIO, http://www.biodiversity.ca)), bluegreenpictures.com pp. **4–5** (David Fleetham); Corbis pp. **23** (Dan Lamont), **29** (Stephen Frink), **39** (DLILLC); Martin Flade/Birdlife p. **33** bottom; FLPA pp. **6** (Minden Pictures/Flip Nicklin), **35** (Imagebroker); Getty Images pp. **13** (The Bridgeman Art Library), **38** (Robert Gray); istockphoto **contents page** bottom (© Marek Mnich), pp. **18** (© Arne Thaysen), **24** (© Benjamin Howell), **27** (© Marek Mnich); Meg Lowman p. **25**; © Wayne Maddison p. **9**; Photolibrary pp. **14** (Oxford Scientific/Harold Taylor), **30** (DEA Picture Library), **31** (age fotostock/John Cancalosi), **33** top (Oxford Scientific/Konrad Wothe), **36–37** (Tom Brakefield); Rex Features pp. **28** (Dana Fineman/Vistalux), **40** (Nature Picture Library/Ben Osborne), **41** (Everett/Animal Planet); Marietta Schupp, EMBL Photolab p. **7**; Science Photo Library p. **12** (Sheila Terry); shutterstock bacckground images and design elements throughout, p. **8** (© Christian Musat/© vnlit/© Martin Valigursky/© jocicalek/© fivespots/© Four Oaks/© Kulaeva Tamara/© hypnotype/© Sailorr/© Lukich/© Arto Hakola); Springbrook Research Centre (Belinda Janke) **contents page** top, p. **22**; Roxanne Steele p. **19**; University of Illinois p. **16**; William Wade p. **15**.

Main cover photograph of BBC TV presenter David Attenborough with a golden eagle reproduced with permission of Rex Features (Nature Picture Library); inset cover photograph of a frilled lizard reproduced with permission of Photolibrary (age fotostock/John Cancalosi).

The publisher would like to thank literary consultant Marla Conn and content consultant Michael Bright for their assistance in the preparation of this book.

Disclaimer

A waterproof identification guide is a very useful thing to have when fish watching!

MEET THE SCIENTISTS

In this book we will meet just a few of the scientists who have dedicated their lives to uncovering the wonders of living things. Some of them are world famous, others may not be so well known. They all do work that is invaluable. It is thanks to people like these scientists, with their boundless curiosity, hard work, and dedication, that we know as much about living things as we do.

LIFE SCIENCES

Scientists who study the living world are called **biologists**. There are many different kinds of biologist. Some biologists look at life on a very small scale to see how living things are put together. Others study the relationships between different life forms. Still others study the way animals behave in the wild.

LIVING WITH CHANGE

Henry Harlow and a team of **researchers** from the University of Wyoming in the United States have been studying the polar bears of Alaska to find out how they are coping with changes to their **environment**. The climate is changing. Each summer the ice sheets where the bears live are shrinking faster than they had before. The bears have to decide whether to stay on land in the summer or go north to try to follow the disappearing ice. Conditions on land are difficult for polar bears. They overheat easily on land and it is hard for them to find enough to eat.

These two scientists are taking careful measurements of a tranquillized polar bear.

The research team track the bears from helicopters and use darts to tranquillize them (put them to sleep for a while). Then they fit the bears with global positioning system (**GPS**) trackers. They also take samples of the bears' breath. "It's a little bizarre because you're in this helicopter with two big bags of polar bear breath," said Harlow. Studying the breath can tell them if a bear has had a meal recently or if it is using up its reserves of fat.

BEING A SCIENTIST

Anne-Marie Glynn is a **molecular** biologist from Ireland who is now working in Germany. **Proteins** and other **molecules** are essential to life. Dr Glynn studied how they work.

Anne-Marie Glynn says that scientific equipment can be simple once you are familiar with it.

<u>Being organized is very important when doing science</u>. Equipment is expensive and has to be booked in advance, for example. Dr Glynn used equipment that let her explore things at high magnification – up to 50,000 times life-size. She says it is like looking at a photograph that you can enter into, to see things "that have never been seen before".

At the same time, a scientist has to be flexible and ready to deal with the unexpected. Dr Glynn makes the point that "one thing you can be sure of in science is that things often don't go exactly according to plan". If you want to be a scientist, she says, then "you need to be inquisitive and to question things – not just believe everything you are told … It's important to believe in yourself and your abilities."

THE DIVERSITY OF LIFE

How many different kinds of living thing are there on Earth? We still have no clear idea what the answer is, and new ones are being discovered all the time.

So far, scientists have named nearly two million plants and animals. People can only guess how many more there may be yet to be discovered. Estimates range from two million to as many as thirty million. One thing we can be certain of is that almost all of them will be insects. Scientists think that insects outnumber everything else by around twenty to one.

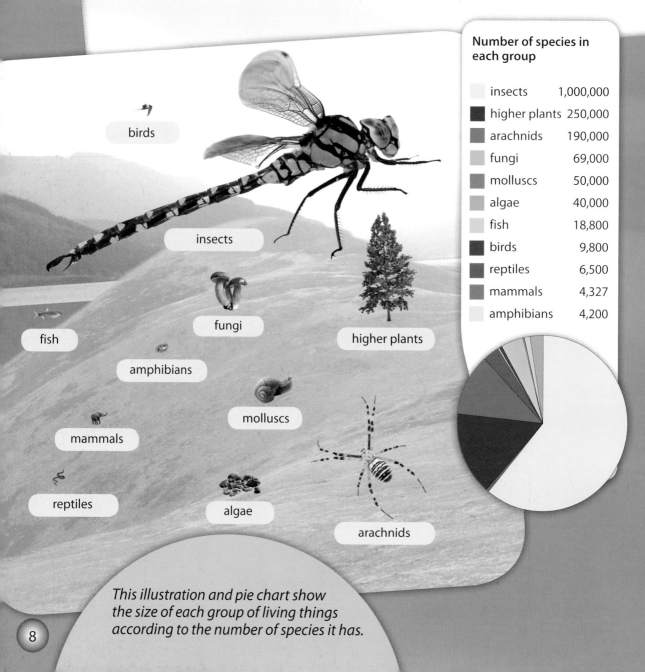

Number of species in each group

insects		1,000,000
higher plants		250,000
arachnids		190,000
fungi		69,000
molluscs		50,000
algae		40,000
fish		18,800
birds		9,800
reptiles		6,500
mammals		4,327
amphibians		4,200

birds

insects

fungi

higher plants

fish

amphibians

molluscs

mammals

reptiles

algae

arachnids

This illustration and pie chart show the size of each group of living things according to the number of species it has.

SPIDER HUNT

In the summer of 2008, Wayne Maddison of the University of British Columbia in Canada led an expedition to Papua New Guinea. He was looking for new types of jumping spider, an animal that fascinates him. "Instead of sitting at the centre of a web, jumping spiders wander around their **habitat** [place where they make their home] and pounce – like cats – on their prey," says Maddison.

On the expedition, the team collected over 500 spiders. They were astonished to discover that more than 30 of them were completely new to science. "Our finding shows that the great age of discovery isn't over by far," Maddison said. He thinks there may be at least 5,000 more types of jumping spiders in the world that are yet to be identified.

These scientists are studying a newly discovered jumping spider (inset).

MORE MAMMALS

It is not just tiny animals such as spiders that are being discovered. Within the last 20 years, over 400 new **mammals** (warm-blooded, hairy animals) have been found and named. That's nearly a tenth of all the mammals known. They include deer, a pygmy sloth, a marmoset, bats, rats, and monkeys. Sadly, over 20 of these new mammals are already at risk of disappearing forever, or **extinction**.

"Most people don't realize this, but we are smack-dab in the middle of the age of discovery for mammals."

Kristofer Helgen, Smithsonian Museum of Natural History, Washington DC, USA

LIFE'S BARCODE

Very often it is nearly impossible to tell what **species** a living thing belongs to just by looking at it. Suppose all you had was a piece of root, or an unhatched insect egg. How would you know what species it was?

Paul Hebert of the University of Guelph, Canada, thought that it would be useful to have a small handheld device to tell you almost instantly what the species was. He got the idea in his local supermarket. He thought about the way supermarkets keep track of everything using barcodes. Perhaps something similar could be done to keep track of the millions of different living things on Earth.

Hebert decided to use **DNA**. This is a type of code that is found in all living things. DNA is passed on from one generation to the next and carries the instructions for constructing and maintaining a new **organism** (living thing). Each species has a different DNA code.

DNA DATABASE

For the system to work, a huge library of DNA samples from the world's living things has to be built up. So far, more than 70,000 species have been catalogued. There are around 10,000 birds in the world. The team hope to have them all recorded by 2011. They believe that barcoding will help to identify up to 1,000 new species of bird.

Species	*Musca domestica* (house fly)
Genus	*Musca*
Family	Muscidae (two-winged flies)
Order	Diptera (two-winged insects, such as flies, midges, and crane flies)
Class	Insecta (insects)
Phylum	Arthropoda (animals with exoskeletons and jointed limbs)
Kingdom	Animalia (animals)

Species may look similar but their DNA barcode helps identify each one.

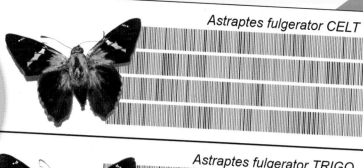
Astraptes fulgerator CELT

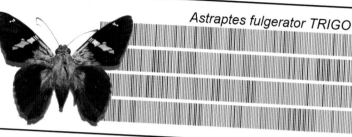
Astraptes fulgerator TRIGO

Bubo virginianus

Tyto alba

"People have watched birds for so long they might think every different tweet has been heard, every different colour observed, but barcoding may prove otherwise."

Paul Hebert

WHAT IS A SPECIES?

The basic unit of classifying living things is the species. Members of a species can breed together to produce offspring that will also be able to reproduce themselves. Individual members of a species may be strikingly different, but they will also have many things in common.

CAROLUS LINNAEUS
and the tree of life

The Swedish naturalist Carolus Linnaeus was the first person to try and organize the huge variety of living things by coming up with a system for naming them and classifying them into groups.

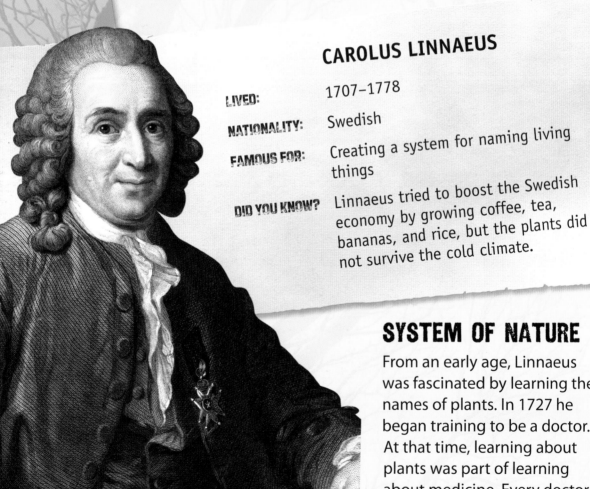

CAROLUS LINNAEUS

LIVED:	1707–1778
NATIONALITY:	Swedish
FAMOUS FOR:	Creating a system for naming living things
DID YOU KNOW?	Linnaeus tried to boost the Swedish economy by growing coffee, tea, bananas, and rice, but the plants did not survive the cold climate.

SYSTEM OF NATURE

From an early age, Linnaeus was fascinated by learning the names of plants. In 1727 he began training to be a doctor. At that time, learning about plants was part of learning about medicine. Every doctor had to know how to prepare medicines from plants.

In 1735, the year Linnaeus finished his medical degree, he published the *Systema Naturae* ("System of Nature"). In it he set out his system for classifying the natural world. The first edition was only a few pages long, but over the years Linnaeus added to it. The tenth edition, published in 1758, took up two volumes.

LINNAEUS'S CLASSIFICATION

At that time, each species was given a scientific name in Latin. These tended to be rather long-winded, however. The tomato, for example, was called *Solanum caule inermi herbaceo, foliis pinnatis incisis, racemis simplicibus*.

Linnaeus had the idea of dividing nature into different groups based on their shared characteristics. He split everything into three kingdoms: plants, animals, and minerals. Kingdoms were further divided into classes, which were split into orders, then genera (singular: genus), and finally species.

Linnaeus greatly simplified the process of naming plants. He gave them each a Latin name in two parts. The first part was the genus, followed by the species. Under the new system, the tomato became simply *Solanum lycopersicum*. Five years later Linnaeus began to extend his system to naming animals, too. Other scientists soon took up the system. It remains the basis of classification to this day.

13

DARWIN AND NEW SPECIES

Why are there so many different species? Charles Darwin (1809–1882) was one scientist who thought about this. He saw that all living things have to compete for resources such as food and water. He also saw that there could be differences between the offspring of each species. These differences might be small but a difference like being able to run faster would increase an animal's chances of surviving and having offspring itself. Over time, a new species of fast runners would appear.

Darwin called this natural selection. Those living things best suited to their environment are the ones most likely to reproduce. This is sometimes called the survival of the fittest. You can find out more about Darwin in *Changing Life on Earth*, another book in this Sci-Hi series.

MICROLIFE

There is a world of living things that is invisible to us because they are too small to be seen with the naked eye. Scientists need to use the powerful lenses of a microscope to examine these tiny **microbes**. The scientists who study microbes are called **microbiologists**.

Although microbes are small, they are hugely important. For example, vast numbers are found in soil and water, where they play a vital part in breaking down and recycling wastes. There are three main types of microbe: bacteria, protistans, and archaea. We will meet the archaea on the following pages.

A drop of sea water may be swarming with microscopic living things.

BACTERIA

<u>Bacteria are the smallest living things that can grow independently and reproduce. They are rarely more than 0.01 millimetre in length.</u> Bacteria can be found just about everywhere. They are in the soil, air, and water, and they live on and in other living things.

No one has any real idea how many different types of bacteria there might be. There are ten times as many bacteria in your body and on your skin as there are cells that you are made of.

In 2008 Professor William Wade (right) of King's College, London, discovered a new type of bacteria living in the human mouth. He said: "there are 100 million [bacteria] in every millilitre of saliva and more than 600 different species in the mouth. Around half of these have yet to be named and we are trying to describe and name the new species."

PROTISTANS

Protistans are bigger than bacteria, but are still too small to see without a microscope. Some can make their own food, like plants, while some eat other protistans. Some protistans live in the bodies of animals, where they may cause diseases.

Carl Woese and the
EXTREMOPHILES

In the 1970s the American microbiologist Carl Woese of the University of Illinois discovered a new group of organisms. Until then they had been neatly classified as bacteria. They were actually so different from anything else that they needed their own category in the living world.

CARL WOESE

BORN: 1928

NATIONALITY: American

FAMOUS FOR: The discovery of the archaea, or extremophiles

DID YOU KNOW? In 1992 the Royal Netherlands Academy of Arts and Sciences awarded Woese the Leeuwenhoeck Medal, the highest honour in microbiology.

ARCHAEA

The archaea (singular: archaeon) that Woese discovered are similar to true bacteria in many ways. However, when Woese examined their **genes** (by which their characteristics are passed from one generation to the next), he discovered that they had some that were also found in multi-celled life forms, and over half of their genes were totally unlike those of any other type of life. <u>The first living things that ever appeared on Earth were probably very similar to the archaea.</u>

The colours of the Morning Glory Pool in Yellowstone National Park, USA, come from the extremophile bacteria living in its hot waters.

LIVING ON THE EDGE

Archaea are often found in the most extreme environments, where no other living thing could survive. Because of this they are also known as extremophiles. They can be found living in some of the most hostile environments on Earth, such as:

- in hot springs or in extremely alkaline or acid waters
- near volcanic vents in the ocean floor where the temperature is close to boiling point
- deep beneath the surface of the Earth in petroleum deposits
- in the stomachs of cows, where they help digest the cow's food.

AN IDEA ATTACKED

Woese's idea was not immediately accepted. Some scientists strongly resisted the idea of adding a new group of organisms. Ralph Wolfe, one of Woese's colleagues, recalled that "many leading biologists thought that Woese was crazy". Although he was ignored and insulted, Woese carried on with his research. It would take 20 years for him to see his idea win acceptance.

GREEN WORLD

Imagine life without wood to make things with, fruit and vegetables to eat, or even the paper this book is printed on. Just about every other living thing on Earth either eats plants or eats something else that eats plants. Plants are of vital importance. <u>The scientific study of plant life is called botany</u>. Scientists who study plants are called botanists.

Botany is a big subject, so most botanists specialize in different areas such as plant **genetics** (the study of genes and what they do) and plant ecology, or how they exist in their environment. Many will divide their time between laboratory work and going out into different habitats to search for new species.

BEING A BOTANIST

Roxanne Steele gave up a career as a mechanical engineer to study plants. The turning point came when she volunteered to help scientists in the rainforest of Costa Rica. "Without delay I quit my engineering job," she says, "began working in a greenhouse, and began taking college botany courses; I have never looked back."

Some botanists study the 5,000 different varieties of potato.

This photo shows Roxanne Steele hunting for Psiguria *in the rainforests of Peru.*

"I want to stress the connection we have with nature and our responsibility to learn about it and preserve it for future generations."

Roxanne Steele

Steele studies a type of plant called *Psiguria*, a member of the cucumber family. No one could decide just how many different kinds of *Psiguria* plant there are. Many change the colour of their flowers and shape of their leaves over their lives. They switch sex from male to female when they grow to a particular size. All this makes it very difficult to identify particular plants. Steele wants to clear up this confusion.

Steele spends a lot of time in the laboratory. However, she says, "Field trips to collect *Psiguria* are the most exciting and the most educational portion of my work … I have travelled to Costa Rica, Puerto Rico, and the Dominican Republic to collect plants … Individuals may be hundreds of metres apart and finding them entails … driving/hiking around searching for them."

In the long term, Steele would like to help educate students and the public about the natural world and the impact we have on it.

plant hunter

George Forrest was born in the town of Falkirk, in Scotland. He was one of the world's greatest plant collectors and explorers. He has been described as Scotland's "Indiana Jones" of the plant world. During the course of his life, he made seven major plant-collecting expeditions, often enduring great hardship. On these journeys, he discovered over 1,200 plant species previously unknown to science.

GEORGE FORREST

LIVED:	1873–1932
NATIONALITY:	Scottish
FAMOUS FOR:	Bringing back over 30,000 different plants, many of which became popular additions to British gardens
DID YOU KNOW?	More than 50 of the plants introduced by Forrest can still be seen at the Royal Botanic Garden at Edinburgh.

In 1891 Forrest went to Australia to try and make his fortune as a gold prospector. After his return to Scotland ten years later, he went to work at the Royal Botanic Garden in Edinburgh. His determination and resourcefulness won him a place on a plant-collecting expedition to China. It was very nearly his first and last trip as the party were attacked by Chinese warriors and Forrest only just escaped.

PIONEERING METHODS

Forrest helped to pioneer modern methods of plant collecting. By getting the help of local people who knew the land well, Forrest was able to collect many more **specimens** than other collectors. Forrest earned a reputation for hard work and dedication over a 28-year career. The careful observations he made of plants were greatly valued by scientists.

"Unlike other collectors at the time, [Forrest] extensively employed local people as collectors. It's a practice we rely on these days ... In addition, the quality of the data he provided for each collection ... far exceeded that of his peers."

Mark Watson, expert on the plants of China, Royal Botanic Garden, Edinburgh

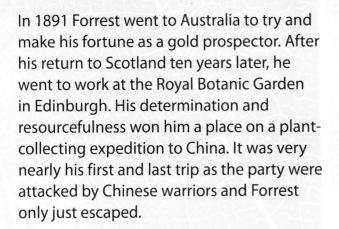

The blue gentian was one of the many plants George Forrest brought back to Europe from China.

Mushrooms
and other fungi

These mushrooms that glow in the dark are found in Queensland, Australia.

Mushrooms used to be thought of as a strange group of plants, but we know now that they are part of a completely different kingdom of life – the fungi. Fungi play a vital role in the living world, helping to break down and recycle dead matter.

HEINRICH ANTON DE BARY

LIVED: 1831–1888

NATIONALITY: German

FAMOUS FOR: Founding the modern science of mycology

DID YOU KNOW? De Bary was one of ten children.

MYCOLOGY

The science of mushrooms is called **mycology** and people who study it are called mycologists. The German scientist Heinrich Anton de Bary is considered to be one of the founders of this branch of biology. He investigated the part played by fungi in plant diseases. He also developed a system of classifying fungi that is still used today.

De Bary was the first person to show that a **lichen** was actually an **alga** (a kind of living thing that makes its own food) and a fungus living together. Lichens are found everywhere, from the frozen Arctic to tropical forests. They succeed by teamwork. The alga captures sunlight, providing a source of food and energy for the partnership. The fungus breaks down rocks to obtain valuable minerals and helps prevent the lichen from drying out. Fungus and alga work so closely together that they could almost be considered a single living thing.

De Bary introduced the term *symbiosis* to describe a partnership between two different living things where both benefited.

MEDICINAL MUSHROOMS

For centuries, mushrooms have been used in folk medicine. Today, scientists are taking a serious look at the real benefits mushrooms might bring.

In 2002, Cancer Research UK published a major study on medicinal mushrooms. The researchers were led by Professor John Smith of the University of Strathclyde. One of the things that impressed them was the way compounds from mushrooms could be used to reduce the unpleasant side effects of treatments for cancer.

The report concluded that medicinal mushrooms could have a real part to play in fighting cancer but there was still a great deal of work to be done.

Mushroom expert David Arora shows some penny bun mushrooms – which are delicious grilled!

Margaret Lowman
"CANOPY MEG"

The topmost part of a rainforest is the canopy. It is a hidden world 30 to 50 metres (100 to 165 feet) above the ground. The canopy is a mysterious place that is hard to reach but which teems with life. Up to nine-tenths of rainforest plants and animals are found in the canopy.

CANOPY SHYNESS

If you could look down on the trees in a rainforest, you would see that there are gaps between them. The trees do not touch each other. Scientists call this canopy shyness and no one knows why it happens.

INTO THE TREETOPS

Margaret Lowman is a pioneer of studying rainforests from up in the treetops. She has made use of hot air balloons, constructed canopy walkways, and used giant cranes to gain access to a part of the living world that few people ever see. Her love of the canopies earned her the nickname "Canopy Meg".

MARGARET LOWMAN

BORN: 1953

NATIONALITY: American

FAMOUS FOR: Developing new methods of studying the rainforest canopy

DID YOU KNOW? Lowman is a single mother who often took her young sons into the canopy with her.

Another way of studying the treetops is by using a canopy raft. This is like a giant net held between air-filled supports that is lowered on to the treetops from a balloon. Suspended on the raft, the scientists can study the trees below them. Using a harness, they can even sleep there!

THE NEXT GENERATION

Lowman is a great believer in sharing her work with the next generation of scientists. She has used satellite technology to beam live broadcasts of her canopy research in the forests of Belize to over 9 million students and teachers in Peru and Panama.

"The raft and hot air balloon are definitely the most fun canopy access tools that I have ever experienced ... The other advantage of the raft/balloon is that these expeditions are usually international in scope ... the value of the data is multiplied by sharing and collaborating."

Margaret Lowman

Insect planet

This giraffe weevil lives in the forests of Madagascar.

About half of all the world's plants and animals are found in the rainforests, and by far the most numerous are the insects. Scientists who study insects are called **entomologists**. Roughly two-thirds of all known organisms are insects, so it is a big field of study!

INSECT EXTINCTION

Insects are so numerous that it is hard to think of them as **endangered** (at risk of extinction). However, they can be. The Rocky Mountain locust was a major crop pest in the United States in the 19th century. Swarms of 120 billion insects stretching over 480 kilometres (300 miles) were reported. Today, the Rocky Mountain locust is probably extinct.

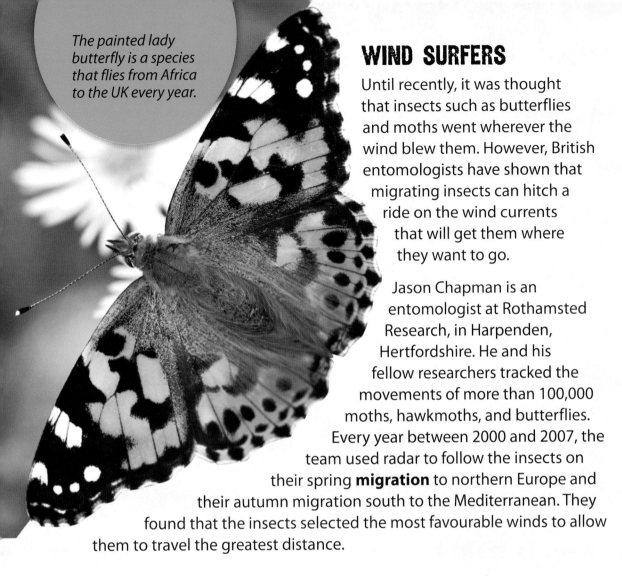

The painted lady butterfly is a species that flies from Africa to the UK every year.

WIND SURFERS

Until recently, it was thought that insects such as butterflies and moths went wherever the wind blew them. However, British entomologists have shown that migrating insects can hitch a ride on the wind currents that will get them where they want to go.

Jason Chapman is an entomologist at Rothamsted Research, in Harpenden, Hertfordshire. He and his fellow researchers tracked the movements of more than 100,000 moths, hawkmoths, and butterflies. Every year between 2000 and 2007, the team used radar to follow the insects on their spring **migration** to northern Europe and their autumn migration south to the Mediterranean. They found that the insects selected the most favourable winds to allow them to travel the greatest distance.

The moths seem to be able to detect the wind's direction and then correct their flight path accordingly. "Insect migration was always thought to be a rather chancy process," says Chapman but "a wide range of insects exert quite a lot of control … and are not, in fact, at the wind's mercy."

FLIGHT SPEED

"Because insects fly slower than birds, they had to evolve a way to increase their speed," says Chapman. They use the wind to do this. Flying over 400 metres (1,300 feet) above the ground, where the wind is fast, the insects can reach speeds of 90 kilometres (55 miles) per hour and cover distances of up to 700 kilometres (435 miles) in 8 hours.

Sylvia Earle
UNDERSEA EXPLORER

Oceans cover around 70 per cent of our planet. Most of the surface of the Earth is hidden beneath water. Just as on land, life is in the oceans. It ranges from microscopic **plankton** to the blue whale, the biggest animal that has ever lived on Earth.

One of the people who have done much to help us learn about the underwater world is Sylvia Earle. She has spent a lifetime exploring and studying the oceans.

SYLVIA EARLE

BORN: 1935

NATIONALITY: American

FAMOUS FOR: Walking untethered (not tied to a lifeline) on the seafloor at a lower depth than any other human being

DID YOU KNOW? Earle has led over 70 expeditions and spent more than 6,500 hours under water.

OIL SPILL

In 2010 Earle gave evidence to the **US House of Representatives** (parliament) on the impact of the *Deepwater Horizon* oil spill in the Gulf of Mexico. "You are the only voice for the ocean that we will hear," the chairman of the committee said when she had read her statement.

DIVING DEEP

Earle was one of the first researchers to make use of scuba diving gear. Ordinary scuba equipment offered no protection against the crushing pressures in the ocean depths. In 1979 Earle made a record-breaking dive down to a depth of nearly 400 metres (1,300 feet). To do this, she wore a Jim suit. This is a metal diving suit that protected her from the pressures outside.

JACQUES COUSTEAU AND THE AQUALUNG

Jacques Cousteau (1910–1997) was perhaps the most famous of all underwater explorers. Together with Emile Gagnan (1900–1997), Cousteau invented a type of scuba (self-contained underwater breathing apparatus) called an aqualung.

Cousteau was a pioneer of underwater photography. He explored the oceans in his ship, the *Calypso*, making award-winning films and television programmes that gave people the chance to see a world that they had scarcely imagined before.

ANIMAL BEHAVIOUR PIONEER

Nobel prize-winner Konrad Lorenz was one of the founders of ethology. This is the scientific study of animal behaviour and how animals communicate with each other.

From a very early age, Lorenz was interested in animals. He had a variety of different kinds of animal, not only the usual dogs and cats, but also monkeys, birds, and fish. Geese, in particular, fascinated him. He kept records of his observations of bird behaviour in a series of diaries.

KONRAD LORENZ

1903–1989

NALITY: Austrian

US FOR: Founding the modern study of animal behaviour

U KNOW? When Lorenz was young, he used to provide care for sick animals from the zoo near his home.

NIKOLAAS TINBERGEN

Lorenz became a doctor of zoology in 1933 and continued to make detailed studies of birds. He set up colonies of jackdaws and geese so he could observe them more closely. In 1936 he met Nikolaas Tinbergen, who became his close friend and colleague. Lorenz often worked with pets and domestic animals. Tinbergen preferred to observe animals in more natural conditions. For their achievements in animal behaviour, the two men (together with Karl von Frisch, a pioneer of bee behaviour) shared the Nobel Prize in 1973.

INSTINCT AND LEARNING

<u>Lorenz saw that behaviour could be divided into two different kinds.</u> There was the kind of behaviour an animal was born with, called **instinct**, and there were behaviours that had to be learned.

Lorenz is famous for the way he showed how young goslings instinctively assume that the first thing they see when they hatch will be their mother. By making sure that he was the first thing they saw, Lorenz made the geese follow him instead of their mother. Visitors to his home soon got used to seeing Lorenz followed by a line of goslings wherever he went.

This frilled lizard may be trying to warn off a predator, a display of instinctive behaviour.

Birds

For most of us, birds are the most familiar of the wild animals that share our world. They are the ones that we see and hear most. They are found in habitats ranging from the frozen Antarctic to forests and deserts. Some soar over the ocean waves. Even in the middle of a city, birds can be found in parks and gardens. <u>The scientific study of these remarkable animals is called ornithology</u>.

ROGER TORY PETERSON

The American ornithologist Roger Tory Peterson was one of the world's foremost birdwatchers. He was also a very talented wildlife artist. Peterson wrote and illustrated a series of field guides to the birds of different regions. The field guides were important in getting people interested in birds. Amateur birdwatchers liked Peterson's system of identifying birds. It was clear and easy to understand.

ROGER TORY PETERSON

LIVED:	1908–1996
NATIONALITY:	American
FAMOUS FOR:	Writing *Field Guide to the Birds*, first published in 1934
DID YOU KNOW?	In 1980 Peterson was awarded the Presidential Medal of Freedom, the highest award that can be made to a civilian in the United States, for his work in environmentalism.

A male bowerbird decorates "a room" to attract a female.

MYSTERIES OF MIGRATION

For some time, ornithologists in Europe were puzzled about where a bird called the aquatic warbler spent the winter months. The bird is endangered (and therefore protected) in its summer habitat in Eastern Europe. The ornithologists wanted to make sure it was protected in its winter home, too.

After five years of investigation, the birds were tracked down to West Africa. Many were found in Djoudj National Park in Senegal. The ornithologist Indega Binda was able to show the European researchers where to find large colonies of the birds within the park. The Europeans used high-tech scientific equipment to track the birds. For example, they compared feathers from birds caught in Europe with those caught in Africa. However, they still needed the expertise of local people such as Indega Binda.

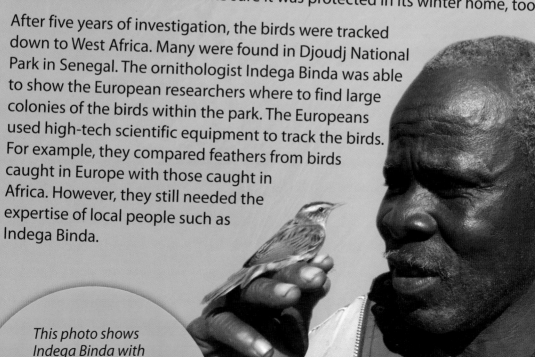

This photo shows Indega Binda with an aquatic warbler.

George Schaller

field biologist

German-American George Schaller is considered to be one of the world's greatest naturalists and one of the finest field **biologists** of our time. He has spent over 50 years studying animals in the wild, observing animals such as lions, pandas, tigers, and mountain gorillas. He is also one of the world's foremost conservationists.

"No one who looks into a gorilla's eyes — intelligent, gentle, vulnerable — can remain unchanged, for the gap between ape and human vanishes; we know that the gorilla still lives within us."

George Schaller

GEORGE SCHALLER

BORN: 1933

NATIONALITY: German-American

FAMOUS FOR: Championing the conservation of mountain gorilllas

DID YOU KNOW? In 1995 Schaller found a herd of Tibetan red deer, an animal that had been thought to be extinct.

The secretive snow leopard is one of the many animals studied by George Schaller.

MOUNTAIN GORILLAS

In 1959, aged 26, Schaller travelled to Africa to study the mountain gorilla. Before he went, little was known about the gorilla. It was thought by many to be a dangerous and savage beast. Schaller showed just how wrong people were about this animal. He revealed it to be a sociable family animal, an intelligent vegetarian that was in far more danger from humans than they were from it.

DIAN FOSSEY

The American zoologist Dian Fossey continued Schaller's work with gorillas. For nearly 20 years she devoted herself to studying and protecting the gorillas of Rwanda and their habitat. Thousands of hours spent with the gorillas helped her to gain their trust. Tragically, her work was cut short when she was murdered in 1985. The crime has never been solved, although many people believe that poachers were responsible.

BIGFOOT

Some people believe that a large, hairy creature that is like a human lives in the forests of the western United States and Canada. They call it Bigfoot or Sasquatch. No Bigfoot remains have ever been found. Most scientists do not believe that it exists at all. George Schaller thinks Bigfoot is a subject worth looking into. "There have been so many sightings over the years," he said. "Even if you throw out 95 per cent of them, there ought to be some explanation for the rest. I think a hard-eyed look is absolutely essential."

LIFE WITH THE LIONS

George Schaller carried out a classic study of the lions of the Serengeti National Park in Kenya. For three years he observed every part of their lives. The result was a unique insight into the lives of animal hunters and their prey.

From 1966 to 1969, Schaller lived in the Serengeti with his wife and two sons. Lions could often be seen prowling around outside the small wooden bungalow where the family lived. The book he wrote about his findings is called *The Serengeti Lion: A Study of Predator–Prey Relations*. It was published in 1972 and is still the prime source of scientific information about African lions.

Other scientists continued the research Schaller began nearly 40 years ago. The offspring of the lions that Schaller watched have been watched, too. One of the main investigators carrying on the work has been Craig Packer. Packer began heading the Serengeti lion project in 1978 and became the director of the University of Minnesota's Lion Research Center.

PRIDE PROTECTION

Scientists have been puzzled about why lions live together in groups, called prides. No other cats do this. For a long time the explanation has been that they increase their chances of a successful hunt by working together. The Lion Research Center has shown that this idea might be wrong.

Lions only hunt together when they really need to – if the prey is a big dangerous buffalo, for example. A female lion can catch a smaller warthog all by herself. It appears that the real reason that lions band together is in defence of their **territory**.

STRENGTH IN NUMBERS

The resources that are vital for lions are food, water, and shelter. <u>The bigger the pride of lions, the more they are able to control and protect these resources</u>. The researchers carried out an experiment in which they played recorded roars of stranger lions to female lions. A single lioness hearing the roar would not approach the loudspeakers, but three lionesses together would. If a trio of roars was played, the three lionesses would wait to get help and five lionesses would approach. This shows how the lions rely on strength in numbers in dealing with a threat.

A pride of lions keeps a watchful eye on their territory.

JANE GOODALL
AND THE GOMBE CHIMPANZEES

One of the world's most famous animal behaviour experts did not go to university. After working as a film production assistant, Jane Goodall travelled to Africa from England in 1957. There she met Louis Leakey. He is a world-famous anthropologist (someone who studies the human species and its ancestors). In 1960 Leakey asked Goodall to study a group of wild chimpanzees at Gombe in Tanzania. She would spend most of the next 40 years there.

JANE GOODALL

BORN: 1934

NATIONALITY: British

FAMOUS FOR: Her pioneering studies of chimpanzee behaviour

DID YOU KNOW? When Jane Goodall speaks to an audience she almost always greets them in "chimpanzee", mimicking a chimpanzee's hoots.

"Young people, when informed and empowered, when they realize that what they do truly makes a difference, can indeed change the world."

Jane Goodall

Chimpanzees use a stick to catch termites. Jane Goodall was the first researcher to see them do this.

Goodall's studies revealed behaviour that had never been observed before. She witnessed chimpanzees using tools. She also discovered that chimpanzees hunt other animals for food. Previously, they had been thought to only eat plants.

CHIMP PERSONALITIES

Goodall saw that each chimpanzee has its own unique personality. Unlike other researchers at the time, she named each of her subjects instead of simply giving them numbers. She saw how chimpanzees would take care of their young, but she also saw how aggressive they could be. "When I first started at Gombe," she said, "I thought the chimps were nicer than we are. But time has revealed that they are not. They can be just as awful."

SPREADING THE WORD

Today Goodall is an active campaigner on behalf of chimpanzees. She travels the world, talking to government officials and meeting young students.

DOCTOR GOODALL

In 1965 Cambridge University awarded Jane Goodall a doctorate in ethology. She is one of only a few people who have achieved this distinction without having studied for a degree first.

LEARNING ABOUT LIFE

Scientists have developed sophisticated tools and techniques for exploring the living world. Science communicators such as David Attenborough have found more and more innovative ways of bringing scientists' findings to us.

DAVID ATTENBOROUGH

BORN: 1926

NATIONALITY: British

FAMOUS FOR: Groundbreaking series of nature documentaries such as *Life on Earth*

DID YOU KNOW? When Attenborough was first offered a job by BBC Television, he had only ever seen a single television programme.

FROM *ZOO QUEST* TO *LIFE*

David Attenborough joined the BBC in 1952 and was soon making a series of wildlife programmes called *Zoo Quest*. For eight years he travelled the world to bring back film of animals in their natural settings. Most people had only ever seen animals in a zoo. They found the programmes astounding. Attenborough, with a degree in natural history, brought knowledge and enthusiasm to his commentary.

With an imaginative, exciting, and scientifically rigorous approach, Attenborough has presented some of the world's best natural history television programmes. These include *Life on Earth*, *The Trials of Life*, and *The Private Lives of Plants*.

EXPLORING THE FROZEN PLANET

In April 2010, at the age of 84, David Attenborough reached the North Pole for the first time. This was just a few weeks after he had visited the South Pole. He said: "to have visited them both within a few weeks of one another is a huge privilege ... having seen what I've just seen – from penguins to polar bears, from the frozen ocean to snow-covered volcanoes – I can't imagine why I've left visiting these marvellous, astonishing and beautiful places until so late in my life."

Conservationist Steve "Crocodile Hunter" Irwin was a popular wildlife film maker before his tragic early death in 2006.

TIMELINE

Follow the coloured arrows to see how some of the ideas and discoveries of biologists influenced other scientists.

Carolus Linnaeus
(1770–1778)

wrote *Systema Naturae*, which set out a method for classifying the natural world.

Konrad Lorenz
(1903–1989)

pioneered the science of animal behaviour and described his findings about behaviour in goslings.

Roger Tory Peterson
(1908–1996)

published the *Field Guide to the Birds* and worked to protect the environment.

Charles Darwin
(1809–1882)

produced a theory of evolution by natural selection and published his findings in a book called *On the Origin of Species*.

Heinrich Anton de Bary
(1831–1888)

introduced the term *symbiosis* to describe a close relationship between two different living things that benefits them both.

Jacques Cousteau
(1910–1997)

tried out the first aqualung, a device that makes underwater exploration possible, and pioneered underwater photography.

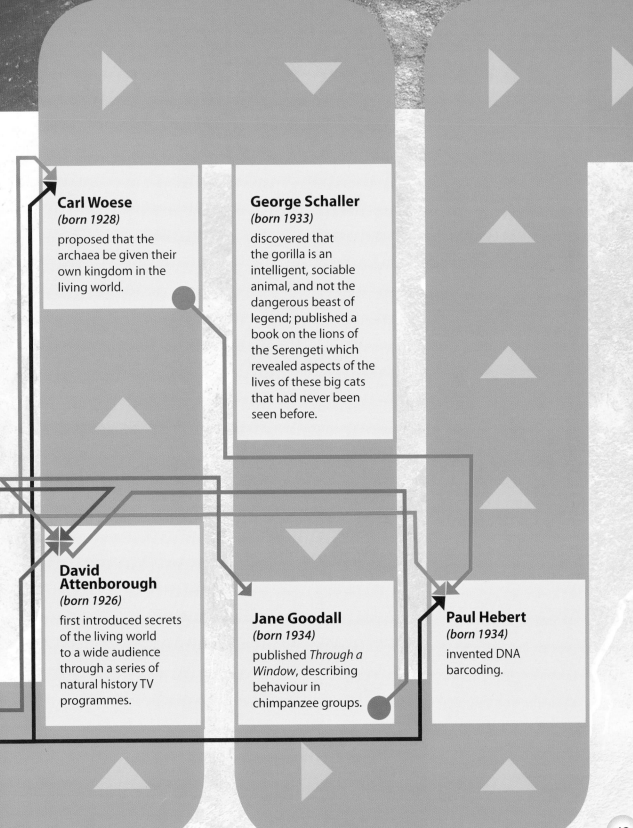

Carl Woese
(born 1928)

proposed that the archaea be given their own kingdom in the living world.

George Schaller
(born 1933)

discovered that the gorilla is an intelligent, sociable animal, and not the dangerous beast of legend; published a book on the lions of the Serengeti which revealed aspects of the lives of these big cats that had never been seen before.

David Attenborough
(born 1926)

first introduced secrets of the living world to a wide audience through a series of natural history TV programmes.

Jane Goodall
(born 1934)

published *Through a Window*, describing behaviour in chimpanzee groups.

Paul Hebert
(born 1934)

invented DNA barcoding.

Glossary

alga (plural: algae) living thing that makes its own food, the way a plant does

biologist someone who studies biology, the science of living things

canopy topmost parts of the trees in a forest

DNA short for *deoxyribonucleic acid*, which carries the information needed for making and maintaining a living thing

endangered at risk of dying out. When species are recognized as endangered, efforts may be made to protect them.

entomologist scientist who studies insects

environment surroundings of a living thing, including all the other living things that share it

ethology the study of the way animals behave in their natural surroundings

extinction disappearance of an entire species of living things from the world when the last members die

gene part of a living cell by which characteristics in a species are passed from parents to their offspring. For example, eye colour is carried in the genes.

genetics the study of genes and what they do

GPS short for *global positioning system*, a means of finding a location on the Earth's surface by using signals from a fleet of satellites

habitat place where a living thing makes its home

instinct type of behaviour that an animal is born with and so does not have to be learnt

lichen organism that consists of an alga and a fungus working together to survive

mammal warm-blooded, usually hairy, animal. Female mammals produce milk to feed their young.

microbe tiny living thing, too small to be seen without a microscope; the more scientific term is microorganism

microbiologist biologist who studies microscopic living things

migration moving from one area to another in search of better conditions. Many animals will migrate to warmer places to escape winter, for example.

molecule smallest unit of a chemical compound

molecular to do with molecules

mycology the study of fungi

organism living thing

plankton tiny plant-like organisms and animals that are found in the sea

protein a food type found in meat, cheese, and beans. Proteins are essential for building and maintaining the body.

researcher someone who finds things out

species group of living things that have many characteristics in common and which can produce offspring successfully

specimen individual animal or plant, or a part of one, that is being studied

symbiosis close relationship between two different species of living thing from which they both benefit

territory area an animal lives in and which it will defend from others

Match the scientist to the science

1 Carl Woese

2 George Forrest

3 Heinrich Anton de Barry

4 Jason Chapman

5 George Schaller

6 Indega Binda

7 Dian Fossey

8 Jane Goodall

(a) botany

(b) entomology

(c) field biology

(d) ethology

(e) microbiology

(f) mycology

(g) ornithology

(h) zoology

Find out more

Books

Animals: A Children's Encyclopedia (Dorling Kindersley, 2008)

Classification of Animals (Sci-Hi), Casey Rand (Raintree, 2010)

Dian Fossey (Levelled Biographies: Great Naturalists), Heidi Moore (Heinemann Library, 2008)

The Diversity of Species, Michael Bright, Heinemann Library, 2008

Face to Face with Lions, Beverly and Dereck Joubert (National Geographic Society, 2010)

Jane Goodall (Up Close), Sudipta Bardhan-Quallen (Viking Children's Books, 2008)

Life in the Undergrowth, David Attenborough (BBC Books, 2005)

Oceans: An Undersea Safari, Johnna Rizzo (National Geographic Society, 2010)

Planet Earth, Alastair Fothergill (BBC Books, 2006)

Plant Classification, Polly Goodman (Wayland, 2007)

Single-celled Organisms (Sci-Hi), Patricia Kite (Heineman Library, 2008)

Steve Irwin (Levelled Biographies: Great Naturalists), Heidi Moore (Heinemann Library, 2008)

What's Biology All About?, Hazel Maskell (Usborne Publishing, 2009)

Who on Earth is Sylvia Earle?, Susan E. Reichard (Enslow Publishers, 2009)

DVDs

Blue Planet, David Attenborough, BBC, 2005

The Jacques Cousteau Odyssey, Delta Home Entertainment, 2006

Last Chance to See, Stephen Fry and Mark Carwardine, Digital Classics/ BBC, 2009

Life, David Attenborough, BBC, 2009

Steve Irwin's Most Dangerous Adventures, Firefly Entertainment, 2002

Websites

www.fi.edu/tfi/units/life
A guide to all aspects of the living world

www.arkive.org
Films and photographs of the world's endangered plants and animals

www.kids.gov/6_8/6_8_science_animals.shtml
A Kids.gov listing of many sites relating to the world of living things

www.canopymeg.com
The official website of Dr Margaret "Canopy Meg" Lowman

www.janegoodall.org
The website of the Jane Goodall Institute, with information about Dr Goodall's life and work

Place to visit

The Darwin Centre
Natural History Museum
Cromwell Road
London SW7 5BD

See leading scientists at work in an amazing glass building housing 20 million specimens from the living world.

Index